From Silence Gathered Book of poems

Introduction

This is a collection of occasional poems written over a period of 30 years. The poems usually arrived fully formed and were put to one side and quite often forgotten. Recently they were brought into the light following three chance encounters, and the images and emotions were gathered up and woven together to make three sequences of poems. The message was conveyed to me "Honour the Promptings of your Soul".

The first sequence I regard as being a "Rosary", made up of beads of memories and images which can be read as one poem, beginning in conflict and traveling through time and place to a final ending.

The second sequence is a collection of fragments, like bits from smashed stained glass windows which were gathered together and reassembled to form a different picture.

The final sequence started off with a rewriting of the Roman Catholic Creed, translated into words I could understand. From there it set off on a search which finally arrives in a Garden of Healing.

Sequence 1 The Rosary

Only a Poem - 18th August 2022

He told me to remain silent
He told me not to put words
Into the poem
hovering
Around me,

But breath and words
Sometimes refuse silence,
Hands still clasped

tightly shut
Begin to loosen their grip
He warned against the
Opening of words
Misunderstood and mysterious,
Words addressed to
A stranger
Who seems so familiar

I protested
Though knowing the truth
I demanded an answer.
What is this?

When seeing your face
Lifts my spirits
And fills me with curiosity
And warmth.
Sometimes you shine a light
That illuminates the rocky path
And walk with me

I protest
And offer as proof
A radiant yellow Peony
And a fragrant white rose
I show you a Buddha
Sitting in the shade of
The golden leafed maple
And leaves of memories pressed between pages .

He listened
He looked me in the eye
And wavering
Softly Instructed
Remember it is only a poem
Only words

We nod
And agree
Only a poem
Only words
We smile .

....

Here with no light to disturb,
no coming and going
no tasks
our faces masked
obscured

Enacting a drama
Futility
poured into empty space

Here is no today
No tomorrow
No forward or back
No should or shouldn't
No place

Is there even a body-
I do not know the answer to that
I touch my face but it tells me nothing
I hold my hands close
To where my heart should be
There IS something stirring
But is it me
Is it mine
I do not know

There are ghosts
phantoms
Fragment of a life lived
Fragments of many lives
Are they mine ?

They seem familiar
Have I heard that voice before?
Have I heard the footfall
The crisp crunching of leaves beneath autumn feet
The flash of yellow and bronze
Kicking leaves and seeing them rise and fall
Dragging the foot across the pavement
Scooping into a pile
Picking conkers
From the spikey cases

Shiny pearls newly fallen
From the sky

It seems familiar
But where does it belong
Whose past is it that seeks me out
Whose memories
Circulate in this dark pulse.

Is this your memory ?

Does this belong to you ?

Who is that child
Who's innocent delight
Can still penetrate this dark place ?

There are many stories lost
So many moments of light
Reduced to nothing
But stirring fragments.

Sometimes the memory so Strong
I hold out my hand
And feel another reaching out towards me
The soft small hand of a child
Snuggling into mine
To guide and protect

……………………………..

A murmuration of memory
Swirling shifting shapes
Gyrations of the ten thousand
Winged creatures
Forming and dissolving
The soft moment
Of vibrations touching the skin
The fluttering of many wings
Engulfing and soothing.

……………………….

Sometimes the hand

Large and rough
Reduces me
Transports me
Despite myself
This hand when it reaches out
Familiar

Whose hand is this that comforts ?

The hand that fends off
Those others that snatch and claw,
And push and pull
Those hands that drag us
point accusingly
And dismiss with
A gesture of finality

……………………………..

They tore away my skin
Flayed alive as they would have said in the history book
But not so dramatic
No blood and guts or tortured screams
Perhaps torn is not the right word
Maybe nibbled or rubbed or eroded
Day by day by day
Year by year by year
A slow process
Unnoticed
Layer by layer removed
Until there was no protection
Nothing to separate inside from outside

………………………………………………

Are you there ?
The kettle has boiled
I've made us a pot of tea
you must be parched
your mouth and throat must be sore
with all that coughing.
Have a sip
Here

I'll hold the cup for you
it's had time to cool.
Let me bring you a flannel
to freshen you up a bit
let me mop your brow

Are you there?
Are you still here?

There are books on the shelves
I think they might be mine
I'm not sure
they look familiar
and there are some letters in a box
the writing looks like mine
they are addressed to you.

The room is a mess
the wallpaper is yellowing
I don't know how.
It's not long since we decorated
remember how you did the gloss
on the doors

Where are you?
Where have you gone ?

Wake up
the babies are crying
they are hungry
they need you.

Can't you hear them
they need a cuddle
they cry so much
Come on wake up
and help me find them
something is wrong
they need their mummy and daddy
Oh thank goodness
there you are
I thought I would never find you
where have you been
come here

let me hold you.

Lets lay down here and rest
put your head upon my chest
let me stroke your hair
let me kiss your lips
for what we were
and then we can sleep.

………………………

Layer by layer removed
Until there was no protection
Nothing to separate inside from outside

…………………….

.Come share this light
Come closer and let me see you
We can rest here
We can tell each other stories and soon there will be sleep
When we wake it will be time for us to begin our search.
But for now we must be still
And wait

……………….

See the flickering light
And the shadows spreading out
Beyond us
Hear the owl's call
As it bounces between the stars
Hold the damp earth
In your hands
Take it in through your skin
Wrap your bones
In its embrace
Call out for an answer

…………………………..

Let me tell you
Of the things I did not know

Things I did not know

I did not know how far we would travel
I did not know we would have to separate
I did not know how deep
I did not know it would be so lonely
I did not know how many pieces
I did not know if it was real
I did not know who had been here before
I did not know if we would ever find ourselves again

……....................

Do you remember
A painted seagull
on the wall
a mattress on the floor
cigarette stubs
scorch marks
on the bare floor boards
A chip paper grease stained -
the sharp smell
of vinegar -
the sound of a car accelerating
an arm protruding
from beneath
an old grey blanket
the heavy rhythmic
breathing
of the sleeper

……......................

Do you remember that dream poem
And that awakening
Can you find those words
In this world full of dust and ash

The room was empty
the house unfound
the floors
blighted
with black fruit
could hold no weight

He stepped in and listening
heard a voice
entombed in time
bound in walls

So Cold
So Cold

A child's empty bed
piled high
with rotted linen

Still I heard
the call
a small voice
Reaching out into the night.

Drawing my hands across the walls
a heart beat
a faint echo
touched my finger tips.

A crack
traced the outline
of a door
to an airless place.

I took a hammer
and broke the seal
I took a hammer
and pounded through
and tore away
bricks and lime.

Let there be light
let there be warmth
Let touch
stir life
into dormant senses
and there shall be hope.

And now when time pauses
I remember

when life was suspended
and began again

Recalling a distant voice
whispering from the tomb
" I am not dead yet
hear me."

…..

Do you remember ?

Wide Eyes

She tugged at my arm
until she found me
she smiled up at me
and held her hand out to me
I held her tiny hand in mine and followed
as she led the way

She showed me the sky is new
and flying ants
streaming out from between the paving stones
She showed me the velvet moss
on the gnarled roots by the stream.

She showed me
still
the crescent moon smiles
like the Cheshire cat.
She knew that I had forgotten

She took me down the road
through the fumes
of cars and wagons and buses
past the dustbins and heaps of wet cardboard boxes
she showed me where she is learning to dance
hopping from shadow to sunlight
she jumped down two steps
and looked to me, in triumph.

We stopped by the stone archway
and she let go of my hand

running through the gap
to the hidden chapel
she turned and smiled
and pointed to the Sky.
It was blue
she knew I can so easily forget.

She hurried through the chapel door
and turning one last time
left the door wide open
for me to follow.
Please do not forget.

Do you remember ?

One room world
One window
looking across
"look there's the little boy
look at him
the red breast
he's come to say hello to me.

And over there
can you see
the lilac tree
white blossomed
like the flowers they laid on his coffin.

He had gone to the shop
I was making jam
the baby played in her cot
there was a knock.

They brought him back
broken
he was so young
and so was I
he whispered to me
it wont be long.

And there are the peonies bursting
and the orange blossoms
of quince

There a carpet of Forget-Me-Nots
Look

He was a young man
stocky of build
just like you.
But he was fair
and so clever
he could turn his hand to anything
the things he could have done.
And down there
behind the hedge
is the river
where I walk

It was 1935
so long ago
We had only just begun
He was so young
and so was I."

Do you remember ?

………………………………………

Walking by the River with Ashley

Days like this are rare
And we know it.

This is a moment to say goodbye
And we will forget we are at work
And stop at Devil's Bridge,
Slurp tea from the van
And sample the bacon sandwiches
mine with Ketchup.

Let me show you the bridge
It is old
So old that no-one knows when it was built
It's always been here
Spanning the rock pools
A reminder of the days
When the Devil had nothing better to do

Than build bridges.

This is where kids jump off
In the summer
Into the deep
They are fearless
And stupid
As befits their youth.
Some are heroes for a moment,
Some never return.

These are the places I belong
This is where I came with Mum and Dad
Where I paddled by the edge
Smelling of malt vinegar.
This is where I brought my children
When they were little,
Smelling of Johnston's baby oil.

If we have such things as roots
Then mine are here
In places like this.
Yours are somewhere else.

Let's walk
I'll show you the path
along the riverbank.
Forget our work
Today is too precious to waste.

See where it flooded last week
the flotsam in the tree tops.
When it's calm like today
it's hard to imagine the power
that rage from those hills.

These are rare days
When the air is like nectar
And the late winter sun
Reflects silver on the rocks
And there is nothing more important to do.

"Well I suppose we'd better get back."
"You know I'll miss you ."

" I should hope you will."

....

Do you remember her ?
Ena

She was one amongst many
Under a childish fringe
a thin sagging face
blemished by lumps
that only old flesh can bear.

I watched her toil
on legs swollen
stretched almost to bursting

This is Ena they told me
" Ena loves music"
they held her hands
and guided her
to an electric keyboard
and slipped a cushion
under the damp pad
of her bottom

Perplexed she touched the keys
and frowned at the abrasive tone
harsh against her own remembered melody

Later we spoke
she told me who she was

She made music in her youth
played piano
while her husband
carved sounds
with the bow of his violin
"he was never very good
but he tried"
she explained

"I won prizes for my dimples
when I was young"

she said with a smile

And I knew this was no lie

Remembering !
Heaven's Vacant Face

Awake to Fugitive need
turning to try to forget
growing spines
through leathered
hide

Closing doors
catching us
when we flee
when we think we know

And soon
it's all over
and beginning again.

Outside the wheels rust
and rutted time
aborts
and sequence
is tied in knots.

I tried to return
to empty space
and seek a home
in those blistered stars
defying
heavens vacant face

....

To The Sea

From my window
I watch her moods.
I see her still calm
her slate gray indifference.
Her rage foaming

agitations spewing and contorting
I see her passions spent
under violent moon

From my door
I hear her songs
her rhymes splashing through youth
her shanties and laments
marking the passing of time's tide.
I hear lovers beckon
I hear the sirens pronounce
a beginning - and an end

On her shores I stand
among the brittle debris
of yesterday
Among the plastic bottles
a discarded shoe
a broken syringe
ribs jutting nameless
carcasses sucked into the mud

In her waters I am seized
and stirred beyond my depth
thrown into darkness and light
swallowed and digested
and broken and mended.
In her fluid womb
I hear a gasping sigh
pronounce
a beginning or an end.

Remember his song ?
My Sweet Lord (thank you George)

Not the Master of the Universe
or the immaculately conceived

Not the God of black and white
or the creator of darkness and light

Not the God who commands us
to kill

those who do not bow
to commands of obedience
here and now
not the Law Maker or the Life Giver

Not the breather of life into silent night

Not the one whose word Is
The all seeing
all knowing
the omniscient
the omnipotent

Not the God of Silver and Gold
of adornment
and rituals
and repentance

Not the God of books
and theologies
and clever ideas
and scribes.
Not the God of Governments
and nations
and holy wars
and processions of the dead

Not the God of deserts
and floods
and commandments.
Of temptations
and devils and demons
and harlots
and nails through hands
and pierced heart.

No
No

Listen

My Sweet Lord

listen

My
Sweet
Lord

………………………………………………

Listen carefully and recall …

My Secret Poet

My secret poet knows no fear
he plucks living words
from the black mud
he grasps the golden fish
he wonders at the silver hues
of night

My secret poet travels through time
he lies on his back
and reaches for the shining
he tastes the delicious fruits of sound

He sees through eyes so old
and reaches out with the soft caress of youth
he knows the mysteries
he solves the riddle
with a single kiss

My secret poet
moves with the stealth of shadows
stalking between the night and day
accepting his wounds
as the consequence of his nature

He rises from the riverbed
and returns
to walk with the living
my secret poet
trembles at the delicacy of knowing
and the wonder of this moment.

And remember how they danced in the waves…..

Birth

We were suspended
in caressing waters
swimming out further than ever before

Side by side
gliding forward
without fear
you carried your unborn child.

The three sisters waiting
our approach
brown skinned and dark eyed
their saris draped the waves.

Knowingly they spoke of birth

the time has come
they whispered
their words
guiding us back to the shore.

………………………………………………

Feel the earth beneath your feet

Spain 1986

Foreign
strange sensuality
everything new
New tastes and scents-
Colours and textures
beckoning
the Sun too fierce to rush

Slowing down
routines that don't need following
regimentation cast away
doing what needs to be done
and no more

White farmhouse in the foothills
fronted by vines
watched over by the thunderous stone
standing in isolation

Dry river bed cut into the gorge
lined with cactus bigger than a man
knotted ropes on either side
where the children played

Burying a jar
among the rocks
it's contents
secret communications
to the future,
a drawing
a pencil
a picture card

Soon after dawn -
tending the terraces
of olives and almonds
turning the ground
behind the clanking
mechanical donkey
it's noise echoing across the valley

White rocks thrown up
from the rust coloured earth
a lizard darting for cover
nameless birds watching
impassive

Later that day
after the siesta
down to the village
Jesus Pobre

The villagers out in procession
brown skinned girls
adorned in ceremonial lace-
men in stubble faced discord
honking down battered trumpets

a happy rabble of possibilities

....

Another time another place.

Garden 1/12/12

I thought I would build a magic garden
from twigs and seed
from gifts and memories.
I sheltered in a circle of willows
beneath a canopy of leaves
perched on an up turned plant pot
drinking coffee from my flask
tilting my head this way and that
seeing
absorbed.

The peony is coming to flower
it's yellow globes
poised
delicious
scoops of
delight.

Thinking no thoughts
I roll a pinch of lemon balm between my fingers
I inhale
and taste
and smile.

I know from other days
there is a path down the centre
of the garden,
I found it when I was digging
and traced the stone edges down the slope.
They were hidden under the weeds and a spade depth of soil.
Two parallel rows of large stones marked the edges and smaller stones, filler between.

Was it you
Stopping to rest your back.
Coughing and spitting
a gob of phlegm on the fresh dug soil.

Packing your clay pipe
and sighing lungs full of smoke
contemplating whether enough had been done
for the day.

Wandering aimlessly around your patch of earth
leaning on your spade
and basking in the thought of all the years
you will work this soil.
Wondering about the past and the future
and the place you stand between them.
Wondering about those who coaxed and tended in the past
and strangers like me in your future
whose face you will never see.

I know you were here
I found the path you set .
And digging
today
the fragments of your clay pipe
returned to the light
as the soil opened and turned to the sky.
I snatched it like a memory, like a found treasure
And put it in my pocket

…..

A place where it began to grow

In Silence Gathered

This is where silence is gathered up
from dark places
and broken landscapes
in silence mourning
the violence that was
and the healing
so long in coming

This is where silence is gathered
and tenderness grows
and warmth in borne
in the dark centre
of a frozen womb

In this silent place
the dead walk once more
not to haunt or curse
but to say their goodbyes
in a sanctified place.

This is where the silence
gathers mothers and fathers
and lost children
and unites them.
Away from their past -
now in warmth
where before
flames kept them apart

This is where silence is gathered up
and tears fall
not like dust and ash
but moist like blood

And the silence finds substance
it lives and breathes
finds shape and colour
and dimensions.

Here crushed lungs
fill once more
and words are borne.
Here silence is gathered
and healing begins.

…………………….

And it all comes round again
Winter gives way to spring
Summer thrives
And seeks rest in Autumn

The clock ticks
………………..
Tick tock
Tick Tock

In the turbulence
catching crumbs thrown
faking deliberation
teasing meaning
from sneezes and tremors
claiming dominion
over seeds that rise
from the earth
and stones that fall from the sky

entwined in brambles
their autumn fruit
black pregnant glories--
those feathers
and claws
and greedy fingers-
raising his head
to look into the starry night
beyond

and once more thinking
of the travelers
deep in the sands
those who step away
from the charted world
swimming in defiance
until the body said
No more
nodding and smiling
an acceptance
to the disappearing skies

and in the deep
he told me of a siren creature
avert your eyes
see no one
hear my words
dance around her
poke fun at her deliberations
and forbidden composure

Throw your words
into her sleep
tell her the ways

of the black thread
absorb her sense
in your patchwork poems

…..........................

the pan was boiling
the tap dripping
the melon on the plate
oozed a sickly sweet goo
the spatula fell
to the floorboards as he brushed past
the green enamel lid
clanked
as he reached in
" Give us this day our daily bread."
the kettle clicked
he inhaled
the rich scent of coffee

…...................................

he smiled
and saw her dance
he sang
no more than a whisper
"Go round, go round little Alice blue gown"
and hummed
where the words deserted him
resurfacing
"I can remember when Alice first came,"
"like a vision she dances"
" she makes me feel just like a man."
"Go round and round
little Alice blue gown"
so many gaps
so many missing words.
He smiled across time
to Alice Blue Gown.

…...

not seeing a thing
no past

no future
no need for stars to guide
turn to the left
always to the left
one step out
hands held high
always to the left.

………………………..…………..

" I knew a man Bojangles
and he danced for me
in worn out shoes."
he walked
in the moonlight
across fields, down lanes
through the valley of shadows
draped in velvet and fur
under the fizz
of electric pylons
a shrieking peacock
in the distance
and meteorites crossing the sky
reminding us we are far from home.

…………………………………….

Tick tock
wrote me a poem
and gave me a name

Tick tock says
"all the poems are written
all the songs are sung"

Tick tock says
"all the leaves are fallen
all the journeys are done"

all his children
have grown
and left him
his mothers and fathers
are dust

all his dreams
have been and gone
and the power
of his youth
is crushed

Tick tock's memory
breaks away
tick tock calls
and silence falls
and there is nothing more
to say

Tick tock
wrote me these poems
and gave me a name.

…...........................

Where do things go
when they go away
do you know the secret
how to make them stay

When things dissolve
before your eyes
and slip from light to dark
things once deeply imprinted
now hardly show a mark

Where do they go
those tears of light
those playful creatures
of the night
where do they go.

He listened to the stories
Swam in the waters
Stepping out onto solid ground
He smiled and spoke
To us
…....................

Before I go
humour me
and let me say
a little prayer for you.

God bless your eyes
your ears
your nose
your touch
and your precious Soul.

God bless you in your joys and sorrows
bless those who journey with you
and bless them when they go their own way.

Bless the days and nights.
Bless you in your fragile humanity
Bless all our days and keep them Holy.

Sequence 2 - Fragments

Waiting
I am waiting for you
to understand something
which I think I know
but which
I think you don't understand

However
I realise that possibly

you do know
and it is me who doesn't
and that you are waiting for me
to understand

I cannot speak of it
because you must
know
for yourself

You cannot speak of it
because I must
know it
for myself

Perhaps neither of us understand

Perhaps both of us Know

…………………………….

Do not close your heart
for it will surely die,
Encased
there will be no joy
and the shadows you run from
will be trapped inside.
Do not close your heart.

…………………………..

We stopped by the stone archway
and she let go of my hand
running through the gap
to the hidden chapel
she turned and smiled
and pointed to the Sky.
It was blue
she knew how easily I forget.

………………………………….

Let's walk

I'll show you the path
along the riverbank.

When it's calm like today
it's hard to imagine the powers
that rage from those hills.

…………………

These are rare days
When the air is like nectar
And the late winter sun
Reflects silver on the rocks
And there is nothing more important to do.

……………………………………

I thought this must be
a room
of lost souls
a place to wait
Grey creatures
shuffling
through passages
stumbling
through time
Drawn to light
fleetingly relived

……………………………………

Fields change
with the seasons
and so do we
we change much more
than the eye can see

I wish I could show you
things from the past
I wish I could do something
to make it last

I'd like to show you
laughter and tears

but they're buried under
all those years.

....

And soon
it's all over
and beginning again.

....

I scooped him up
and held him close
absent-mindedly
touching my cheek
against the warm
crown of his head
inhaling the sweet scent
of his wispy blond hair

Holding him tight
feeling his soft comfort
swaying gently
to a tune only I could hear
looking deep
deep into his eyes.

....

Late winter
clear day
afternoon sunlight through the window
streaks of dirt on the outside
condensation on the inside
Shining on the chimney stack
of the house across the alley
pots outlined in silver
stand like chess pieces
against the sky

....

Before we meet again
you will have
left your Self behind,

the one you were
the many you were
and those you strove to be.

…………………………….

Blackbird

Sometimes the day begins
in the echoes of the song
the blackbird sings,
and the silken light
from retreating night
bathes the newborn day.

Sometimes the weight
of nights dark crush
hangs heavy on the day,
and no sweet song
or golden light
can take that night away.

Sometimes I look around me
at souls on bended knee
searching for a better place
A prayer to set them free.

……………………………..

the floors
blighted
with black fruit
could bear no weight

……………………………………….

Distance

Because you kept your distance
I never knew who you were
you remain a puzzle

Because you changed
your shape

and took the form I needed
I could never grasp your being

Because it all seemed
so full and easy
and natural
I dreaded there must be deceit
Yet still I believed

………………………………

The ghost dance of youth
the primal trance
of night and fire.
Fixed in a music
that throbs and shivers
through every atom.

…………………………………….

First word

Each word uttered is the first word
the created
the light

each word uttered is the last word
the end
the dissolution
the darkness
And there are so many words.

……………………………………..

I wanted to say
What I do not know

I wanted to walk
Where I cannot go

I wanted to describe
what I cannot see

……………………………………

He told me
the truth of our story
we meet
we join
we create
we dissolve.

…………………………….

We know our emptiness
we know our solitude
we wait and dream
of the flowering
and another beginning

……………………………………………
One word

Let us start with Love.
what twists and turns we have
with this insignificant little word
Four letters
one syllable
one exhaled breath
which slips through the lips
in a second.

……………………………………………

Who unfolds in a smile
And spreads wings
Around tears
Of sorrow.
………………………….

I looked to the North and the east and the west and the south
To the heavens and the earth

……………………………….

The secret revealed
but no words could be found
nothing to bring shape to what was seen
nothing for us to do

to break the illusion.

....

You found shelter
in maternal arms
I faded into the shadows

....

Watched over by the thunderous stone
standing in isolation
Dry river bed cut into the gorge
lined with cactus bigger than a man
knotted ropes on either side
where the children played.

....

White rocks thrown up
from the rust coloured earth
a lizard darting for cover
nameless birds watching
impassive

....

And the silence finds substance
it is gathered
in your walk
in your eyes
and fingers
It gathers on the slope of your shoulders
and the soft tone of your voice
it dwells on the considered words
you chose.

....

In the silver light
inhale the sombre joy
of the white lily
beneath the fragrant stars
of honey suckle

Stay in this peace

……………………………..

One more time
tread lightly across
those fragile fibres
Walk with me

………………………………………

Your silence
means you are never quite real
though you are more
much more
than a shadow
on the wall

………………………………

The walls
draped
with curtains of lime
Mineral veils
that glistened
in the arcs of light

Explosions of fern
growth
thriving
drawn by the light
their innate urge
to break
the dormant waiting

………………………………

There was a flood
time passes
there was a city
full of strangers
time passes

There was a time

when truths were pondered
and throw to the wind
and dispersed

……………………………

Old Grey Beard
sits in the Willow Shelter
in the garden we created
he sees through silence

Today he held out his hand
to share
his sweet yellow heart
as an offering
as a gift
as a poem.

…………………………..

Don't
stand in defiance
of the sparking stream
don't
deny this life
as an empty dream

Don't
say it doesn't matter
when you know
it does

Don't
get in the way
of your life

Sequence 3 - The Creed

Shadows

Before your sun is eclipsed
by the
by the shadows
of your
unlived life

Before you give up

seeing the shapeless creatures
disfigured, and distorted
clawing
at the heart
of life

Know these things
are real
but they are not
all there is

There is so much healing
to be done.

………………………………………..

Creed (30th November 2018)

Bow to the heart of the Creator
the one who lives in all things
in the wonders
of the Heavens and the Earth

Bow to the Son of the Creator
to the one who lived
his Divinity
and walks amongst us
who speaks of the Holiness
within us
and the blessings
we can find
in all creation

Bow to the Holy Mother
who grew within the mystery of conception
and formed the body and soul
in the waters
of her womb.
Through her touch
she taught of a love
that the creator of the stars
could never have known

Bow
to the homeless wanderer
who spoke of truths
no-one could hear -
to our brothers sisters
who are judged
whose suffering
goes unheeded

Bow
to the one who journeyed

into the heart of darkness
who guided those
lost in the shadows
and rose again
with word and spirit
undefeated by death

Bow
to the spirit that moves with us
who animates our living days
who weaves our lives
with the wisdom
of the Holy ones
who walked before us

Bow
to the one
who sees us
in our strengths and weaknesses
who is our father
mother brother sister
who is our child
who is the stranger
who passes us on the street

Bow
to the one
who guides and forgives
the one who illuminates
our path
into the future.

…………………………………..
Whatever passes along the paths of the seas

Out of sight
or a glimpse then gone
existing in another element
fluid

Subjected to tides and storms
draining from the hearts of mountains
freezing
thawing

traveling over the earth
gushing through unseen caverns
bubbling up
bringing life

Moving to the sea
drawn by moon
lifted and rolled
churned
foaming

Paths of the seas
never the same
only a moment

who can perceive
what passes
through those pulsating currents
who can trace
the moment
of those paths of the sea.
……………………
The Way - 22 October 2018

If you are satisfied
to know we have
no destination

If you are happy
to carry on
with me
when we don't know
where we are
or why

If there is no goal
other than
the journey
we can walk the way
together

…………………..

In These Waters

These waters
are calmed now
there are no currents
to move you
nothing to take you
here or there
no place we need to go

I will rest now
here
join me
between this beginning
and the end

Here we will talk
and listen
and wait.

....

What is?

What is poetry?

The joining of the world
and the soul
germinating into words

What is God?

The meeting of the world
with the soul
transformed into love

What is love?

The meeting of the world
with the Soul
engulfing all creation.

Who am I?

body and soul
germinating in words
transforming in love
engulfed in creation
basking in Unknowing.

………………………….

Walking
Keep on walking though you don't know where
walk through wakefulness
and dream
continue
keep going
though there is no destination
no arrival

Walk the paths
that grow beneath your feet
tread through morning dew
listen to the crunch
of fallen leaves
look through the canopy
of branches
cradling the sky

You will see the altar
in a clearing
a ruined chapel
whose walls crumbling
and entwined
shelter you
from the wind
and frame the vastness
of stars
as you lay down to rest

Know the sacred heart
that shines in this place
know the unseen
companions
who bless this altar
and prepare for your arrival

Take a single flower
to place on the altar
as a gift
to those who passed before
and those who
will walk this path
in future days

And when you are renewed
continue on your way.

....

Claire's Garden (May 2017)

When we see
the bees   go to and fro
from   flower to flower
and the   young birds
    are   hopping about

When a frog soaks up the afternoon sun
    in the   lap of the Buddha

We know
at this moment
all is well.

....

It is
it is not
it is and is not
it is both
and neither

It is real and fantasy
it is living breath
it is an idea

You can touch it and feel it
though it is not here

it is always here

It can never be touched or felt
it can never be known
it always remains

It is
It is not
It is

....
Lady of the flowers

I could see She was troubled
I watched her
infected by the beautiful sorrow
she carried

She visited the graves
and laid flowers
by the headstones

Sometimes she knelt
speaking
in those whispering tones.

I wanted to go to her
and hold her hand and comfort her
I wanted to weep with her
as she knelt
head bowed

I wanted to help her carry
all that sorrow

We became lost
but not forever

She found me
Sitting
by the newly dug grave
She wiped the tears from my eyes
and reminded me

She told me
there are people like us
who are lost
who can only ever be strangers
whose task is to nurture the dead.

Finding companionship
in the echoes of other lives
we lay flowers
on the graves
of strangers

....

Peony

It is soft and bright
formed
in winter sleep
awaiting

unfolding
its tight centre
spreading
yellow petals
opening
in renewed light

new
and precious
now
a brief time
shining
Through The Cracks of This Twilight World
6 October 2013

When we are taken
off guard
and think there is
no-one there
to make us
accountable
for our words.

We speak
from the depths
of our heart.
Before the witness
the judge and jury
of our mind
shames us
once more into
silent retreat.

We stumble
with the innocence
of an unbroken child,
or the wisdom
of one who knows
just how short
life can be
and how silence
can last
for all eternity.

We speak without
a thought
of consequence
and shine
a light
through the cracks
in this twilight world.

………………………………..

I was with you - 29 June 2018

I remember
we sat on the bench
at the bottom of the garden
under the damson tree
you could hear the ocean
in the distance

We smoked your duty free cigarettes
you watched the bats swoop
low below the branches

catching midges

The hedgehog
appeared on time
scuttling around the lawn
meandering in search of something
always hurried
always urgent

As the night grew darker
you looked up at the stars
It was a clear night
and as we looked
more and more
appeared
constellations you recognised
but could not name
formed before your eyes

You say I wasn't there
but I sat with you
my arm draped across your shoulders
like brothers,
I was the bat and the damson tree
the busy hedgehog
I was the smoke you breathed out
and the stars in the night sky
and the breaking waves
on the shoreline

I was with you that night
And if you can find your way back
when ever that might be
wherever you are
I will be there
waiting.

……………………………….

You cannot find it where you are looking
yet will never find it
unless you search
if I were a poet
I would say it will find you

only when it is your time
but I am no poet
and all I can do is shrug
and lie on my back
watching the clouds
forming and dissolving
and hope that they can
pray me to a better place

……………………………….

It was twilight
the lane almost gone
hedges on either side
overgrown merging
ancient blackthorn
ladened with sloe
food for the birds
thorny
scratching engulfing

……………………………….

Garden Moments

19 November 2018

Late in the day
black sky
penetrated by red sunset
in the distance we see
a rainbow
touches
the darkening town
…………………..

Winter has not yet
taken hold
across the earth -
confused primulas
their yellow flowering
premature
in their mistaken
springtime.
………………………….

The branches alive
with Blue Tits
a Robin
perched
on matchstick legs
inspects
the newly dug soil
……………………………..

Buddha statue
sits
by the rock
orange bell tangles
of Nasturtiums wilt
tired of reaching out
Now shedding their seed
for tomorrows
they will never know
……………………….

The solitary maple
naked branches
their adornment
fallen
carpets the slope
with red and gold
………………………….

22 November 2018

The twigs
taken from another garden
I cut them
and removed the thorns
I poked them into
the soil
Now I can only wait
and see
………………………………

The spring bulbs
poke through into the light

not knowing
of the coming frosts
I dig away the soil
of the embankment
removing roots
and broken glass
……................................

18 October

Now the time
feeling the chill
sneaking through the night
the weakening light
of day
the whole earth sighs
through the golden leaves
…............................

Time
time
time moving
limited now
you abandoned to your nature
I leave you
to your undoing
there is nothing more
I can do
for now
....

December garden moments

14 December 2018

Door aslant
held shut by wire twisted
wound around
a screw -
inside a stack

of empty plant pots
a net of dried onions
hanging from a nail
a rusty saw leans
against the wooden slats
of the shed wall
……………………………..

Frost crunching under foot
untouched
by the weak December sun
icing on the grass
and the low spread
of foxglove leaves
a Blackbird
swoops
and pecks
the amber rot
of a fallen apple
……………………..

Battered old wheelbarrow
dented and encrusted
empty rigger gloves
palms up in gesture
skeletal
towering
thistle headed Cardoon
…………………..

A stranger I had forgotten
a shrub planted two years ago
bland and disappointing -
It calls out
above the browning mush
of fallen leaves
it sings the sweet song
of it's first flowering
offering the lemon scent
from it's tiny white heart
……………………………..

I saw a pallid crescent moon
in the tired blue winter sky -
then walking further
I turned
and saw the sky transformed
the foaming waves
rippling across
a perfect blue sea
illuminated by the setting sun.

………..................

Prayer flags frayed
incense burning
offering rising
rolling with the breeze
twilight birdsong
the cry of seagulls
the smell of sandalwood

……....…...............

Waterbutts and buckets
topped with ice
green toupée of moss
capping a rock
ferns flattened
by recent wind and rain
the velvet buds
of next year's
starry magnolia.

……..................................

Garden moments

22 February 2019

Red Admiral
first butterfly of the year
lands
on stones
by our feet
we rest

in this shaft of light
....

Another day
a different butterfly
yellow Brimstone
criss crossing
above the garden
goes
into the woods

....

Big bees
little bees
feasting in the warmth
inspecting
the winter honeysuckle
disappearing
into the yellow centre
of daffodils

....

The Blackthorn
tall and slender
white blossom
Blue Tit hangs
from the feeder
pecking at fatballs
Robin
hops
onto the seed tray

....

Late February
should still be winter
today
warm as May
everything out of sequence

Old men
shake their heads
and warn
of frosts

and freezing winds
yet to come.
……................

Barrowing mushroom compost
up the hill
slow
deliberate
stopping to catch my breath
sweat from my brow
stings my eyes
……....................

Sunlight through Hazel
Catkins dripping
incandescent
Crow
screeches
from the treetop
……....................

Listen

Everywhere

birdsong

……....................

Tap tap tapping
woodpecker
searching
somewhere
near

Garden Moments

March 2019

Tall brittle
stems
giant thistle heads
lying spent
across the path
……....................

Last weeks storm
tore loose
her roots
she hangs
suspended
between
heaven and earth
…............................

A stone
resting on a stone
beckons
to a bygone
day
…............................

White magnolia
stars
Buds
on fruit bushes
Michaelmas daisies
spreading roots
underground
…....................

Time for dividing
one
split
into many
separate
beginnings
…....................

Empty pots
and seed trays
waiting
to be filled
with
tomorrows
...…................

Digging up Foxgloves
digging up Evening Primrose

digging up Teasle
digging up Feverfew
we plant again
in a different
garden
…..........................

emptying
teabags
into a bowl
to feed
the soil
…................

Water trickles
from embankments
after
heavy rain
planting
must wait
….......................

She planted a tree
by the window
when he died
spring
Cherry blossom
renews her
ambivalent memories
…..........................

A clock face
without hands
a mute witness
to passing
seasons
…...................

Plum tree
blossom
one
solitary
bee
….......................

The rotting timber
shed
broken to pieces
soon
will be
consumed
in flames
……….............…

A thousand
blossoms
how many
will
come to fruit
....

Garden Moments

31 March 2019

He sits
on a twig
raising his head
his song
an exaltation
……............…

He hasn't seen me
sitting
silent
watching
he preens
and flutters
in the hawthorn
……....................

A movement
brown bird
upturned tail
Jenny Wren
by the purple primula
moving

in the shadows
of the prayer flags
….....…..........

Shouting
clapping
the thud of a football
sharp sound of
referee's whistle
from across
the railway track
….................

Soon be time to cook
leg of lamb
for Mother's Day
I break a twig
of Rosemary
and set off home.
…............................

Skip full of rubbish
plastic tubs
and broken glass
protruding
through
twisted wires
the battered wooden
handle
rusty treasure
trenching spade
…..............................

Sweetpeas
nurtured
on the kitchen table
now
a greenhouse feast
for a hungry mouse.
…..............................

Black crow
sits
on the pinnacle
swaying
in the wind
....

Setting sun
behind giant
Leylandii
pools of fire
shine through
its darkening presence
....

Wandering
aimlessly
wondering
what to do
next
…..........................

Let me ask
Mr Mouse
why did you
nibble holes
in the fingers
of my rubber gloves
…......................

Pear tree
now in blossom
black and white
cat
on evening patrol
…...................

Chill wind
on my face
bag of rhubarb
by the gate
free
to anyone
who wants it

....

Crocosmia
rampant
knotted clusters
of bulbs
Uprooted
to quell
their exuberance
before they
engulf
....

They cut down
the veil of trees
along
the railway embankment
exposing
a world
where time
still counts
.....…...........

Bark
peeling
off the stump
forms pictures
of mountain ranges
and jagged paths.
....

Sirens
approach then fade
Wind
blowing through
the trees
sounds
like waves
on the ocean
....

Wind breathes incense
right
then left

then towards me
now
a horizontal flow
now
a spiral of
gray kisses

........…...........

Who would have guessed
so much life
in this nameless
moment

....

Potting
Evening Primrose
and clumps of Aster
Robin watches
by my feet
Drone of a plane
somewhere
above the clouds

....

19 April 219

Good Friday

Today
they remember
once more
our crucified Christ
Today
an Orange Tip
butterfly
graced
my awakening
garden.

....

21 April

I strike a match
to light
the incense
Woodpigeons
call
messages
only they can
understand
……………………

One crimson bud
Rhododendron
unfolding
gulls squabble
overhead
……………

Early morning
opening
the polytunnel door
to let in
the sweet
new morning
air
……………………

Two Black Crows
peck
at the shed roof
I glance away
for a moment
when I turn back
they are gone
………………………………

May Garden 2019

This apple tree
he planted
for the birth
of his first son

Now
the season
is right
the Séamus tree
heavy with blossom
....

Fionn

I grafted
a new tree
onto a root stock
on the day he was born
In his second year
we see
it's first bloom
on slender stem
….................

Rainfall
transforms
dry soil
Now moist
gathering
receptive
…........................

Always being born
always dying
always dying
always becoming
Always
....

When I go
it remains
It calls out to me
I listen
and
recall
....

Some seeds
burst into light

Others linger
in darkness
till the time
is right

....

It was warm
and bright
when I planted them
Now the cold
leaves them
sagging
there future
uncertain

....

What roots
unseen
will grow
what seeds sown
will never rise

....

Two blackbirds
in a hurry
land by my feet
A Thrush
with beak full of worms
disappears
behind the Foxgloves

....

If midges were stars
sitting here
I would be
the centre
of a vibrating universe

....

Listening
understanding
the offering
of this beauty
should be shared

before time passes
and it is gone
forever

....

You missed the Flowering

You missed the flowering
the waking from winter.
I wanted to tell you
You must come.
You must see that brief awakening
the dormant beginning again
That unique cycle
Soon to be passed.
Soon to be history.

I wanted you to see the aquilegias
in their blues and pinks
some plain faced
others subtle in their beauty.
The tall foxgloves
swaying gently

I wanted you to see the Yellow Peonies
Those flowers I see as yours
they were brought from a lost garden
and were planted anew
in freshly dug soil.
There they stand
strong and proud

I wanted you to see the tall
slim plum trees
with starlight blossom
and the pear
and the cherry trees
abundant.

I wanted to show you
I wanted you to see

....

A walk in Remembrance

Weary from coughing
limbs aching and weak
from the virus
sweating with the exertion
walking slow
to the waiting garden

Crossing the threshold
it embraced me

Welcoming
it guided me to a seat
to catch my breath

I could see how time
ever changing
had turned the seasons
leading us
into spring

Slowly slowly
I followed the
meandering path
taking in the
fresh yellow primulas
the white star shaped
petals of magnolia

Seeing the fading blossom
on the Blackthorn

The Buddha
sitting solid
serene
among the early flowering Hellebores
and the unfurling ferns
carpeted in fallen
Maple leaves
The hedge alive
with expectant hungry birds

I filled the feeders
and sitting waited
watching
as they darted to the seeds

Above my head
the searching breeze
swayed the wind chimes
a sad reminder
of those who are not here.
....

Ragged Prayer

Ragged prayer
ragged love
frayed
weathering storms
frost and sun
torn through nights and days
dispersing
responding
hearing birdsong
fluttering
beckoning
sagging
singing
to you

listening to your song

Ragged prayer
Ragged Love

Printed in Great Britain
by Amazon